Moment Aufnahmen

Jena

Moment Aufnahmen

Hans-Werner Kreidner

Jena

Die schönsten Seiten ■ At its best

SUTTON

Impressum

Sutton Verlag GmbH
Hochheimer Straße 59
99094 Erfurt
www.suttonverlag.de
Copyright © Sutton Verlag, 2014

ISBN: 978-3-95400-331-0

Gestaltung und Satz: Sutton Verlag
Übersetzung: Easytrans24.com, Hamburg
Druck: Florjančič Tisk d.o.o. / Slowenien

Bildnachweis

Alle Fotos stammen von Hans-Werner Kreidner, Jena. Ergänzende Aufnahmen lieferten:

Stefan Harnisch/Zeiss-Planetarium Jena: S. 43 o.
Paul Melzer/Ernst-Abbe-Stiftung Jena: S. 54 u. l.
Horst Ertel/Sielmanns Natur-Ranger, Team Jena: S. 71 u. r.
Uwe Germar/m4medien, DVD-Produktion „Durch Jenas Gebirge":
    S. 78 m.
Ewa Kryston: S. 79 u. r.

Einleitung | Introduction

Die kleine Großstadt Jena, mit 105.000 Einwohnern die zweitgrößte Stadt Thüringens, zeigt mit ihrer traditionsreichen Uni, dem ältesten Planetarium und der reizvollen Natur viele Gesichter. Jena besticht durch seine Lage im mittleren Saaletal, eingebettet in eine südländisch anmutende Landschaft, und trägt eine Reihe feiner Beinamen: Universitätsstadt, Zeiss-Stadt, Saalestadt, Stadt der Sieben Wunder, Leuchtturm, Stadt der Wissenschaft, Lichtstadt, Boomtown …

Ende des 9. Jahrhunderts als „Iani" erstmals erwähnt, erhielt die Ortschaft um 1240 Stadtrecht und als „Jene" war sie lange ein beschauliches Wein- und Ackerbauernstädtchen. Eine Folge der Reformation war die Gründung der Universität. Der Entscheidung von Kurfürst Johann Friedrich I., 1548 in Jena eine Hohe Schule zu gründen, die zehn Jahre später zur Universität erhoben wurde, verdankt die Stadt ihre wissenschaftliche und wirtschaftliche Entwicklung. Um 1800 erlebte Jena eine unglaubliche Blütezeit als ein geistig-intellektuelles Zentrum Europas, einer der Hauptorte frühromantischer Debatten. Große Geister wie Goethe, Schiller und Fichte zogen einen Kreis junger Intellektueller an, der als die „Jenaer Frühromantiker" in die Geschichte einging. Nicht wegzudenken aus Jenas Kulturgeschichte ist Goethe, zumal der Dichterfürst die Stadt als geistige Ergänzung zum Weimarer Hof verstand. Für Goethe war sie einst ein „liebes närrisches Nest", später eine „Stapelstadt des Wissens". Goethe schloss hier den Freundschaftsbund mit Schiller, der die meiste Zeit seines Lebens in Jena verbrachte, sich hier vermählte und zum Professor an der seinen Namen tragenden Universität wurde.

Untrennbar mit Jena verbunden sind Ernst Abbe, Carl Zeiss und Otto Schott. Das Dreigestirn legte Mitte des 19. Jahrhunderts den Grundstein für die industrielle Entwicklung der Stadt. Der Physiker Abbe revolutionierte die Fertigung optischer Instrumente, schuf die Grundlagen des wissenschaftlichen Mikroskopbaus. Mit Zeiss und Schott begründete er das, was Jena heute als Stadt des Lichts berühmt macht.

Alle großen Persönlichkeiten, die hier Spuren hinterließen, von Luther bis zu den Künstlern der klassischen Moderne, machten Jena zu dem, was es heute ist. Sie prägten unverwechselbare Markenzeichen der Stadt wie den querdenkerischen Geist. Dieses spezielle Flair ist allerorten zu spüren. Mit 25.000 Studierenden an Uni und Fachhochschule ist die lebendige Wissenschaftsstadt eine Studenten-Hochburg.

Although it is the second largest of Thuringia's cities, Jena is relatively modest in size, with a population of just 105,000 people. It is, however, a city with many different faces – a historic university, the world's oldest planetarium and some of the most stunning countryside, are just some of the many reasons to visit. Nestling in an almost Mediterranean landscape in the middle reaches of the Saale valley, Jena goes by many names: university city, city of Zeiss, city in the Saale valley, city of Seven Wonders, city of science, city of lights, boomtown Jena …

First documented as "Iani" at the end of the 9th century, Jena was granted municipal rights in 1240 and developed in subsequent years into the modest farming and wine-growing town of "Jene". One of the consequences of the Reformation was the founding of the university and it could safely be said that the town owes its scientific and economic development to the decision in 1548 by Elector Johann Friedrich I to establish a seat of learning in the town. Around 1800, Jena experienced a rise to prominence, emerging as an intellectual centre in Europe and an important setting for the debates of the forerunners of the Romantic Movement. Great thinkers of the time such as Goethe, Schiller and Fichte attracted a circle of young intellectuals, later to become known as the "Jena Romantics". A key figure in the cultural history of the city is, of course, the great poet Goethe, who saw Jena as a spiritual extension of the court at Weimar. It was here that Goethe met and became close friends with Schiller, who spent most of his life in Jena, marrying here and becoming a professor at the university which today bears his name.

Other names inextricably linked with Jena are Ernst Abbe, Carl Zeiss and Otto Schott, the triumvirate of distinguished scientists who, in the mid-19th century, laid the foundations of Jena's industrial development. Abbe, an eminent physicist, revolutionised the manufacture of optical instruments and was involved in developing the first scientific microscope. Together with Zeiss and Schott, he helped to earn Jena its title "city of light".

Countless major figures, from Luther through to the artists of Classic Modernism, have left their mark here, shaping the city of Jena we see today – a place stamped with its own distinctive personality and a healthy disrespect for conventionality. With 25,000 students enrolled at its two universities, Jena – this exciting city of science – remains a vibrant centre of academic excellence.

Wahrzeichen

Jena zwischen Historie und Hochtechnologie: Uni-Gründer „Hanfried" und das mittelalterliche Johannistor vor dem allgegenwärtigen JenTower, dem modernen Wahrzeichen der Hightech-Metropole als Ausrufezeichen. Der Turm spiegelt das liebenswerte Jena. Als natürliches Wahrzeichen erhebt sich der markante Gipfel Jenzig, eines der „Sieben Wunder" Jenas, über der Saale.

Jena – a city where historic and high-tech rub shoulders: the statue of "Hanfried", founder of the university, and the medieval Johannistor gate, dwarfed by the mighty JenTower – a bold, symbolic expression of the city's high-tech credentials. The lighthouse reflects Jena's many charms. Among the natural landmarks of the city is the distinctive Jenzig Mountain, one of the "Seven Wonders" of Jena, which overlooks the Saale river.

Marktplatz

Umsäumt von historischen Bürgerhäusern und moderner Architektur, lädt eine ganze Reihe traditionsreicher Lokale mit Freibewirtschaftung in Jenas „guter Stube" zum Verweilen ein. Das über Jahrhunderte erste Haus am Platz, „Zur Sonne", ist frisch saniert. Der Bismarck-Brunnen erinnert an den Besuch des einstigen Reichsgründers 1892.

With a mix of historic townhouses and more modern architecture, the market square has a number of traditional pubs and restaurants in which to linger a while and enjoy Jena's warm hospitality. For centuries the only house on the square, "Zur Sonne" (the cheerily-named "Sun House") has recently been renovated. The Bismarck Fountain was built to commemorate the visit to Jena in 1892 of the founder of the German Reich.

  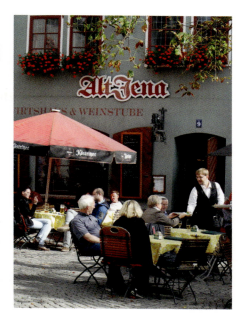

Mit Schwert und Lutherbibel steht mitten auf dem Marktplatz auf hohem Denkmalsockel Kurfürst Johann Friedrich der Großmütige, auf dessen Initiative die Universität gegründet wurde. Aufgestellt wurde „Hanfried" zur 300-Jahr-Feier der Uni, 1858. An der Nord-Ost-Ecke lenkt ein stattliches Bürgerhaus mit hohem Fachwerkgiebel die Blicke auf sich, das heutige Stadtmuseum war über sechs Jahrhunderte das Wohnhaus des Marktmüllers. Am Markt 11 leuchtet hoch oben ein Stadtwappenmosaik mit Erzengel Michael, dem Stadtheiligen, als Drachentöter. Der Jenaer Markt gehört zu den schönsten geschlossenen Marktplätzen Thüringens. Im Zweiten Weltkrieg entstandene Lücken sind seit den 1990er-Jahren geschlossen. Der Neubau neben dem Rathaus wird wegen seiner knalligen Farben als „Papageienhaus" bezeichnet.

In the centre of the market square on a high pedestal stands the figure of the Elector John Frederick the Magnanimous, clutching a sword and a Lutheran bible. It was on his initiative that the university was founded. The "Hanfried", as this statue is affectionately known, was erected in 1858 to commemorate the 300th anniversary of its foundation. An attractive building in the north-east corner of the square is the grand townhouse with high half-timbered gables which today houses the city's museum. For over six hundred years it was the residence of the market miller. Reflecting the light high up on the building at number 11 is a mosaic coat of arms depicting the Archangel Michael, patron saint of the city, as a dragon-slayer.

Altstadtfest und Töpfermarkt

Weihnachtsmarkt

Lichterglanz und Budenzauber: Der Jenaer Weihnachtsmarkt präsentiert sich als Klassiker, seit 1803 verbürgt, gilt er als ältester in Thüringen. Traditionell trägt das Turmblasen vom Rathaus zur einzigartigen Atmosphäre bei. Übers Jahr beliebt sind Volksfeste. Dann wird der Markt zur Bühne. Einer der schönsten Töpfermärkte in Thüringen ist zum Mekka der Keramikliebhaber geworden. Die jahrhundertealte Tradition des Töpferhandwerks passt bestens in die historische Altstadt.

Twinkling lights and the festive charm of Christmas stalls: Jena's Christmas market is a classic – established back in 1803, it is thought to be the oldest of its kind in Thuringia. Every day a traditional trumpet fanfare from the town hall announces the opening of the market, adding a delightful touch to the uniquely festive atmosphere. Another popular attraction are the festivals which take place throughout the year, when the marketplace becomes a large open-air stage. One of the best pottery markets in Thuringia has become a mecca for fans of ceramics.

Eine Besonderheit der Rathaus-Kunstuhr ist das Figurenspiel „Schnapphans", eines der „Sieben Wunder" des alten Jena. Zu jedem vollen Stundenschlag schnappt der Narr „Hans von Jehne" vergeblich nach der goldenen Kugel eines Pilgers, während ein Engel das Glöckchen läutet. Das originale Schnitzwerk von 1480 ist im Stadtmuseum zu sehen.

An interesting feature of the astronomical clock on the town hall is the figure of "Schnapphans" (Snatching Hans), one of the "Seven Wonders" of old Jena. As the clock strikes the hour, the fool "Hans von Jehne" attempts to grab a golden sphere dangled by a pilgrim. The original carved figures of 1480 are on display at the city museum.

Rathaus

Das altehrwürdige Jenaer Rathaus, ein stadtbildprägendes Doppelhaus, gehört zu den ältesten Deutschlands. Der gotische Bau, 1368 erwähnt, wurde auch als Kaufhaus genutzt. Eine offene Halle diente dem täglichen Markt für Bäcker, Fleischer, Tuchhändler. Erhalten ist ein Arkadendurchgang. Der barocke Mittelturm wurde 1755 aufgesetzt. Im Obergeschoss ist die Ratsdiele sehenswert.

The ancient city hall of Jena, a distinctive semi-detached building, is one of the oldest such buildings in Germany. This Gothic structure, first documented in 1368, was at one time used as a department store. An open hall provided a space for butchers, bakers and drapers to ply their trade every day. The baroque central tower was added in 1755. The council chamber on the upper floor is of particular interest.

Stadtmuseum

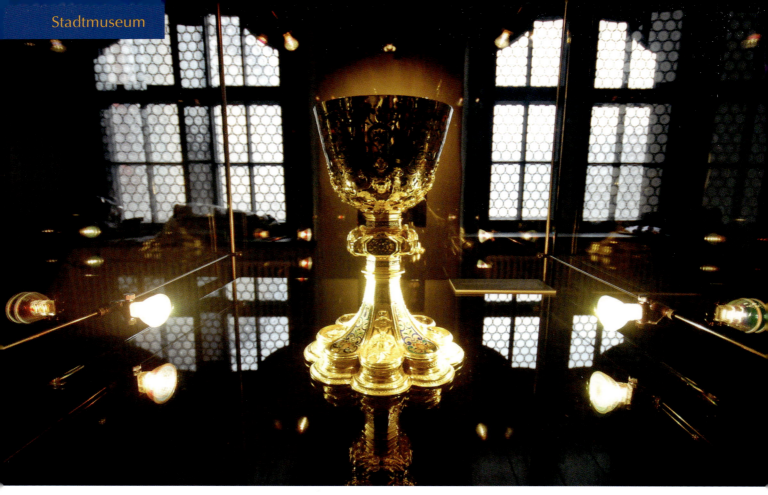

Eine Zeitreise durch Jenas Stadtgeschichte ermöglicht die „Göhre", ein stattliches spätgotisches Bürgerhaus am Markt mit Fachwerkgiebel. Die historische Bohlenstube beherbergt Goldschätze wie das Prunkstück eines Abendmahlskelchs von 1570. Im Kellergewölbe ist das Mittelalter zu bestaunen: die originale Plastik des Heiligen Michael aus dem 13. Jahrhundert, einst an der Stadtkirche angebracht, und die „Jenaer Pietà".

For a fascinating journey back in time through the Jena's history, a visit to the "Göhre" is recommended. The historic parlour of this fine late Gothic townhouse on the market square, with its half-timbered gables, houses an exhibition of gold treasures – its centrepiece a magnificent communion goblet dating back to 1570. The vaulted cellar has medieval treasures to admire, such as the original 13th century sculpture of Saint Michael which once adorned the city church, and the "Jena Pietà".

„Sieben Wunder" hat Jena. Das Stadtmuseum zeigt auch „draco", einen siebenköpfigen Drachen, den Studenten 1600 fertigten. Einst war es ein Studiennachweis, die lateinischen Namen aufzusagen: „Ara, caput, draco, mons, pons, vulpecula turris, Weigeliana domus – septem miracula Jenae". Mit originalen Teilen der alten Weinstube „Göhre" eingerichtet ist das Museumscafé „Philisterium". Zur Schatzkammer der Stadtgeschichte zählt ein begehbarer Himmelsglobus nach dem Vorbild von Erhard Weigel. Die Kunstsammlung der Stadt Jena zeigt in der Galerie bedeutende Sonderausstellungen klassisch-moderner Kunst.

Jena is famed for its "Seven Wonders". Visitors to the city's museum can see one of them at first hand: "draco" – a seven-headed dragon made by students in 1600 to refer to when reciting the Latin names of Jena's famed Seven Wonders: "Ara, caput, draco, mons, pons, vulpecula turris, Weigeliana domus – septem miracula Jenae". The museum's "Philisterium" café is decorated with original fittings from the old "Göhre" hostelry. A definite highlight of the collection is an enormous walk-in globe modelled on Erhard Weigel's original. Jena's art gallery features special exhibitions of important works of Classic Modernism.

Stadtspeicher | Tourist-Information

Die Tourist-Information am Markt 16 avanciert selbst zur Sehenswürdigkeit. Das Domizil „Stadtspeicher" ist ein Zeugnis jahrhundertealter Bautradition. Hinter der imposanten, 16 Meter hohen Stahl-Glasfassade verbirgt sich eines der ältesten Häuser Jenas. 1384 erbaut, ist es einer der wenigen erhaltenen mittelalterlichen Ständergeschossbauten. Der aufwendig restaurierten Fachwerkkonstruktion wurde die hypermoderne Fassade vorgeblendet, da es keinen historischen Beleg gab. Das schmale Haus besteht aus zwei separaten Bauten: Vorn befindet sich das Lager- und Kontorhaus, dahinter das Wohnhaus mit massivem Erdgeschoss und zwei Fachwerketagen. Die Holzstube in Blockbauweise war der einzige rauchfreie warme Raum. Mittelalterliches Wohnen ist in diesem Schmuckstück erlebbar. Der Fenstererker kragt zum Hof aus. Im Atrium kontrastieren Historie und Moderne eindrucksvoll. Wegen seines Alters und der fast vollständig denkmalgerecht wiederhergestellten Holzkonstruktion ist der Stadtspeicher einzigartig.

The tourist information office at Number 16 on the market square is rapidly becoming a tourist attraction itself. This former residential building, known as the "Stadtspeicher", is a fine example of a centuries-old building tradition. Concealed behind the building's impressive 16-metre high steel and glass facade is one of the oldest houses in Jena, built in 1384 and one of the last remaining medieval structures of its kind. In the absence of any accurate historical information as to how the facade would have looked, it was decided to conceal the carefully-restored half-timbered construction behind a superimposed ultra-modern facade. The narrow building actually comprises two separate houses – at the front is the storehouse and office, whilst the rear part contains the living quarters, comprising a large ground floor area and two half-timbered upper floors. The block-built wooden parlour was the only warm room which was smoke-free. This unique architectural gem provides a real insight into what everyday life was like in the Middle Ages. An oriel window juts out over the courtyard. The atrium is an impressive mix of old and modern. The "Stadtspeicher" is a truly unique piece of architecture, not only because of its age but also because of the faithful reproduction of its wooden construction.

Das farbliche Erscheinungsbild der Glasfassade am „Stadtspeicher" ändert sich je nach Tageszeit und Standpunkt. Die holografisch-optischen Elemente von Schott leuchten in allen Spektralfarben. Die Hologrammscheiben sind eine Hommage an Optik, Licht und Glas – Jenas Identität.

The colours of the Stadtspeicher's glass facade change according to the time of day and the viewer's perspective, with each of Schott's individual hologram panels reflecting the various colours of the spectrum in myriad ways. The creator's deliberate choice of materials for this eye-catching frontage pays homage to Jena's long association with optics, light and glass – so much a part of the city's identity.

Stadtkirche „St. Michael"

Sie ist eine der größten Hallenkirchen Thüringens, die spätgotische Stadtkirche „St. Michael", erbaut zwischen 1380 und 1556. Das prächtige Brautportal gilt als Unikat der Architekturgeschichte. Die kreuzbogengeschmückte Altarunterführung gehört ebenfalls zu den „Sieben Wundern" Jenas. Sie diente als einzige Zufahrt zum Zisterzienser-Nonnenkloster. Die Türmerstube in der barocken Haube ist begehbar. Die Turmuhr besitzt als Besonderheit mittelalterliche Einzeigeruhren.

The late Gothic city church of "St Michael", built between 1380 and 1556, is one of the largest hall churches in Thuringia. Its magnificent bridal portal is unique in architectural history, whilst the arched passageway under the chancel, with its decorative groined arches, is another of Jena's famed "Seven Wonders". At one time it provided the only access to the Cistercian nunnery. The tower room in the baroque-style cupola is accessible to visitors. The clock tower is unusual in having medieval one-handed clocks.

Kurios: Die Stadtkirche „St. Michael", wichtige Luther-Erinnerungsstätte, beherbergt seit 1571 die originale Grabplatte des Reformators. Das 1548 gegossene Bronzeepitaph, für die Wittenberger Schlosskirche bestimmt, gelangte durch Kriegswirren nur bis Jena und verblieb hier. Von 1522 an war Luther elf Mal in Jena, mal inkognito, mal als heftig streitender Reformator. Zwei Mal predigte er von der hiesigen Kanzel. Jena gilt als wichtigster Druckort der Luther-Bibel.

The city church of "St Michael", an important memorial site of the great Reformer, has been the site since 1571 of Luther's gravestone. The bronze epitaph made in 1548, was originally intended for the Schlosskirche in Wittenberg but, in the chaos of war, it only reached as far as Jena, where it was to remain. From 1522 Luther came to Jena eleven times and he preached twice from this pulpit. Jena was the most important centre for the printing of the Lutheran Bible.

Johannistor

Das Johannistor ist das einzig erhaltene der drei Stadttore. Der 1304 erwähnte und fast 30 Meter hohe Torturm besitzt über dem fünften Geschoss einen Umgang. Der Aussichtserker „Käsekorb" diente der Stadtwache. Der Pulverturm mit seiner Bastion an der Nord-West-Ecke der mittelalterlichen Befestigung war der stattlichste und stärkste. Mit dem rekonstruierten Wehrgang über der Stadtmauer bildet er ein idyllisches Ensemble. Beim Nachtwächtergang mit Laterne und Hellebarde durch schummrige Winkel sind schaurige Geschichten zu erleben.

The Johannistor is the only one of Jena's three city gates still in existence. First mentioned in 1304 and standing almost 30 metres tall, this handsome gate tower has a parapet around its fifth storey. Nicknamed the "cheese basket", the oriel window was where the nightwatchman kept an eye on the city's goings-on. The Pulverturm (Powder Tower), with its bastion on the north-west corner of the medieval fortifications, was the strongest and most impressive. Together with the reconstructed battlement walkway it forms an idyllic ensemble. A walk with the night watchman – complete with lantern and halberd – through the dimly-lit corners of this part of the city is a chance to hear spine-chilling stories from days gone by.

Pulverturm

Haus „Zur Rosen"

Das Uni-Gasthaus „Zur Rosen" schmückt eine prachtvolle originale Renaissancefassade. 1561 erwarb die Universität den Rosenhainschen Weinbauernhof, der neben dem Kollegienhof der einzig authentische Ort der Gründungsphase der Alma Mater Jenensis ist. In der Schenkstatt wurde 1570 das Rosenprivileg zum Ausschank von Bier und Wein gewährt. Heute ist es ein Haus für den wissenschaftlichen Nachwuchs der Uni.

The student pub "Zur Rosen" boasts a splendid original Renaissance facade. Acquired by the university in 1561, the premises – originally "Rosenhain's winery" – is the only surviving building (apart from the Kollegienhof) from the time of the founding of the Alma Mater Jenensis. In 1570 it was granted the right to serve beer and wine. Today this renovated building is frequented by a new generation of young scientists.

Johannisstraße

Die Johannisstraße war für den Fernhandel die West-Ost-Hauptverkehrsader. Nach Norden zweigt die Jenergasse ab, einer der ältesten Straßenzüge. Ein hohes Ackerbürgerhaus von 1583 beherbergt die „Weintanne". Wie im Studentenclub „Rosenkeller" in der Johannisstraße laden hier alte Gewölbekeller stilvoll zu Speis und Trank. Einst waren alle Häuser mit Gewölben unterkellert. Beliebter Blickfang sind die „Tanzenden Mädchen" vor der Goethe-Apotheke.

The street known as Johannisstraße was an important west-east route for foreign traders. Branching off northwards is the Jenergasse, one of the city's oldest streets. A tall farmer's townhouse, dating from 1583, now houses the "Weintanne" restaurant. Like the "Rosenkeller" student pub in Johannisstraße, its fine original vaulted cellar provides a stylish setting in which to enjoy a drink or a bite to eat. At one time all houses had vaulted cellars. Outside the Goethe-Apotheke chemist stands a particularly charming statue – the delightful "Tanzende Mädchen" (Dancing Girls).

JenTower

Der JenTower prägt das Stadtbild wie kein anderes Wahrzeichen. Es ist das höchste Bürogebäude im Osten Deutschlands, mit Antenne erreicht es 159 Meter. Die Universität nutzte den umstrittenen Bau von 1972 bis in die 1990er-Jahre. Seit 2000, nach Rundumsanierung und Aufstockung, leuchtet an dem Firmensitz eines Software-herstellers für Internethandel der Schriftzug „Intershop". Liebevoll wird der Turm auch „Keksrolle" genannt. „Neue Mitte" heißt das Center am Fuß des gigantischen JenTower, der sich im einstigen Zeiss-Forschungsbau „b 59" spiegelt. Es ist Jenas zweithöchstes Bürohaus, 65 Meter hoch. Seit zehn Jahren gibt der Bau der Stadt sein modernes Gepräge.

Soaring to a height of 159 metres (including the antenna), there is no more potent symbol of the city of Jena than the JenTower, the highest office building in the east of Germany. This controversial structure was used by the university from 1972 until the 1990s. Since 2000, following major refurbishment and extension, it is now the head office of the e-commerce software company Intershop Communications. The JenTower has acquired various affectionate nicknames over the years, including "Keksrolle" (biscuit packet)! Located the foot of the massive JenTower is the centre known as the "Neue Mitte", here reflected in the former Zeiss research building (known as "b59") which, at 65 metres, is Jena's second highest office block. For the last ten years it has given the city an ultra-modern look.

Neue Mitte

Aussichtsplattform JenTower

Hoch über Jena. Im JenTower schwebt der Gast in doppeltem Sinn auf höchstem Niveau. Außergewöhnlich ist das „Scala" im 27. Geschoss, das zweithöchste Hotel Deutschlands, einzigartig auch das Turmrestaurant. Überwältigend ist das Panorama von den beiden Aussichtsplattformen auf der 28. Etage. Aus 128 Metern Höhe schweift der Blick nach Westen über den Campus Ernst-Abbe-Platz zum Forst (oben). Von hier aus bietet sich eine traumhafte Aussicht auf Stadtkirche, Rathaus, Kernberge und den markanten Gipfel des Jenzig nach Osten (links). Die Kuppel des Zeiss-Planetariums ist zu erkennen, bei guter Sicht die Leuchtenburg über dem Saaletal im Süden. Es ist nicht zu übersehen, dass Jena eine Stadt im Grünen ist – eine der am schönsten gelegenen Großstädte.

High above Jena – the JenTower offers visitors a high-quality experience ... and that does not just mean the view! Extraordinary features include the "Scala", Germany's second highest hotel, on the 27th floor and the unique tower restaurant, whilst the panorama from the viewing platform on the 28th floor is truly breathtaking. From a height of 128 metres the eye sweeps west across the university's Ernst-Abbe-Platz campus to the forest (above), whilst the view eastwards takes in the city church, the city hall, the Kernberge mountains and the unmistakeable peak of the Jenzig (left). It is also possible to make out the dome of the Zeiss Planetarium and, on a clear day, the Leuchtenburg castle overlooking the Saale river to the south. From this perspective you realise just how many green spaces the city of Jena has – in fact, few other cities can boast such a stunning location.

Collegium Jenense

Der Kollegienhof ist die Urstätte der Alma Mater Jenensis. Im malerischen Innenhof des Collegium Jenense wird in einer freien Dauerausstellung die Geschichte der Universität lebendig. Im einstigen Dominikanerkloster gründete der sächsisch-ernestinische Kurfürst Johann Friedrich I. auf Anraten Melanchthons 1548 eine „Hohe Schule", die 1558 zur Universität erhoben wurde. Prachtstück ist das große Ernestinische Wappen am Treppenturm der einstigen Kirche. Grabplatten von Professoren schmücken den Torbogen. Keine andere deutsche Uni besitzt einen solchen Ort wie den Kollegienhof, wo akademisches Leben vom Mittelalter bis heute pulsiert.

The "Kollegienhof" is the heart of the Alma Mater Jenensis, the city's original university. A permanent exhibition in the picturesque courtyard of the Collegium Jenense traces the history of this prestigious academic institution. The first academic establishment was established here in 1548 by Johann Friedrich I, on the recommendation of the theologian Melanchthon, in what had originally been a Dominican monastery. University status was then awarded in 1558. A particularly fine feature is the large Ernestine coat of arms on the stair tower of the former church. The Kollegienhof is completely unique among German universities in being able to boast a thriving academic tradition stretching from medieval times right up to the present day.

Stadtführungen im Kostüm sind beliebt. Bei Zeitreisen in die „Stapelstadt des Wissens" ist viel Spannendes über das alte Jena zu erfahren. „Gründerjahre in Jena – ein Spaziergang mit Carl Zeiss' Gattin Ottilie" führt zu den ersten Zeiss-Werkstätten, zur Universität und Sternwarte. Besucher lauschen Geschichten um Ernst Abbe und Otto Schott. Die Figur „Pedell" weiß über weinselige Studenten und berühmte Professoren zu berichten.

City tours in costume are always popular and there several to choose from. Take a journey back in time and learn all about the exciting history of old Jena on the "Stapelstadt des Wissens" tour. Alternatively, the "late 19th century in Jena – a walk with Carl Zeiß' wife Ottilie" takes you to the original Zeiss workshops, the university and the observatory. As part of the tour, visitors can hear stories about Ernst Abbe and Otto Schott. Those walking with the "Pedell" (the town's beadle), on the other hand, can look forward to hearing tales of tipsy students and famous professors.

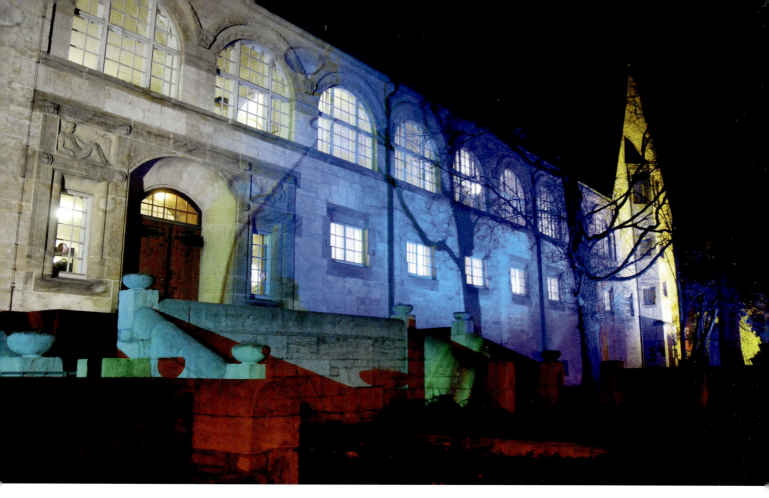

Das Universitätshauptgebäude, eines der bedeutendsten deutschen Hochschulbauten, wurde 1906 anstelle des alten Schlosses nach Plänen von Theodor Fischer errichtet. Namenspatron Friedrich Schiller hielt hier als junger Professor der Philosophie 1789 seine berühmte Antrittsvorlesung. Das Gebäude vereint historische und moderne Formen des Jugendstils mit symbolischen Elementen. Den Turm zieren Plastiken der Tierkreiszeichen.

Designed by Theodor Fischer, the main university building – one of the most important higher education establishments in Germany – was built in 1906 on the site of the old castle.
It was here in 1789 that the young professor of philosophy, Friedrich Schiller (the university's patron), delivered his famous inaugural lecture.

Friedrich-Schiller-Universität

Bedeutende Persönlichkeiten studierten und lehrten an der 1558 gegründeten Uni. Der vierflügelige Bau hat einen großen Innenhof. Die Aula schmückt Ferdinand Hodlers berühmtes Gemälde „Auszug deutscher Studenten in den Freiheitskrieg von 1813". Ernst Abbe, in der Aula steht seine Büste, war hier Dozent für Mathematik und Physik.

Many important people have studied and taught here at Jena's fine university, whose origins date back to 1558. The building has four wings and a large courtyard. The main hall has several interesting features, including Ferdinand Hodler's famous painting "Auszug deutscher Studenten in den Freiheitskrieg von 1813" (Jena Students Depart for the War of Liberation 1813) and a bust of Ernst Abbe, who taught mathematics and physics here.

Fürstengraben

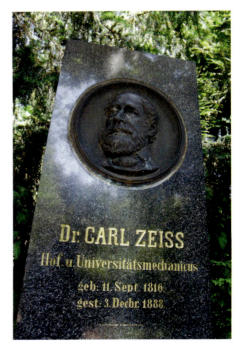

Entlang der Via Triumphalis am Fürstengraben, gegenüber dem Goethe-Ginkgo (oben), reiht sich Denkmal an Denkmal, sie würdigt Professoren des 18./19. Jahrhunderts. Heinrich Luden, politischer Philosoph, war einer der geistigen Väter der Jenaer Urburschenschaft. Kugelförmig die Hommage an Ernst Abbe, der durch seine berühmte Lichtbrechungsformel den Bau von Mikroskopen wissenschaftlich revolutionierte. Das Grab von Carl Zeiss steht auf dem historischen Johannisfriedhof.

Opposite the Goethe-ginkgo tree (above) one side of Fürstengraben – a route known as the "Via Triumphalis" – is lined with numerous monuments commemorating professors from the 18th and 19th centuries. The political philosopher Heinrich Luden was one of the founding fathers of the original student fraternity of Jena. A large, ball-shaped monument commemorates Ernst Abbe, whose famous discovery of the refraction of light led to a revolution in microscope manufacture. The grave of Carl Zeiß is in the historic Johannisfriedhof cemetery.

Löwenbrunnen

Am Breiten Stein, dem kleinen Platz mit Löwenbrunnen von 1702, mündet die Oberlauengasse in die Saalstraße. Das Haus von 1655 trägt zur Zierde einen zeittypischen Fachwerkerker (rechts). Das Trebitzsche Haus besitzt die einzig erhaltene Rokokofassade. Das Platanenhaus ist das letzte an der einstigen östlichen Stadtbefestigung. Schmuckstück des gastlichen Weinbauernhauses „Im Sack" ist die Bohlenstube von 1596 (rechts). Ein Sitznischenportal führt auch zur Kneipengalerie „Zur Noll" in der Oberlauengasse.

At the junction of Oberlauengasse and Saalstraße is the tiny square known as 'am Breiten Stein', its centrepiece the attractive Löwenbrunnen (Lion Fountain) erected in 1702. The house dated 1655 has a decorative half-timbered oriel window, typical of the period (right). Nearby Trebitzsche Haus has the city's only surviving rococo façade, while the Platanenhaus is the last remaining part of Jena's eastern defences. Another sight not to be missed is the convivial wine-grower's house "Im Sack", with its centrepiece wooden parlour of 1596 (right). Passing through an ornate portal with niched seating, you enter the galleried "Zur Noll" pub and restaurant in Oberlauengasse.

Zwischen Saalstraße und Unterm Markt

Frommannsches Anwesen

Das Anwesen des Verlegers Carl Friedrich Ernst Frommann (1765–1837) am Fürstengraben war seit jeher ein Forum des geistigen Austausches Intellektueller. Schelling, Tieck, Fichte, die Brüder Humboldt, Brentano und Hegel trafen sich hier. Vor allem Dichterfürst Goethe war häufiger Gast und genoss die ungezwungene Geselligkeit. Um 1800 versammelten sich hier führende Autoren der Klassiker und Romantiker zu den „Frommannschen Teestunden". Heute ist der Frommannsche Garten eine Oase zum Entspannen inmitten der quirligen Stadt. Nahe der Universitätsbibliothek lassen sich Studierende gern von den Musen inspirieren.

The former home of the publisher Carl Friedrich Ernst Frommann (1765–1837) on Fürstengraben has long been a forum for intellectuals to exchange ideas. Schelling, Tieck, Fichte, the Humboldt brothers, Brentano and Hegel met here. Goethe, Germany's greatest poet and scholar, was a frequent guest here and enjoyed the freedom of the hospitality extended to him. Around 1800, a circle of leading Classical and Romantic authors would gather regularly "to take tea at Frommann's". Today the garden provides a welcome oasis amidst the noise and bustle of the city. Students near the university library seek inspiration from their muses.

Botanischer Garten

Der Botanische Garten der Universität, zweitältester in Deutschland, seit 1586 „Hortus Medicus", beheimatet 12.000 Pflanzen aller Klimazonen. Arboretum, Alpinum und Gewächshäuser mit Kakteen-, Palmen- und Tropenhaus sind eine Attraktion. Im Victoriahaus gedeiht die Amazonas-Riesenseerose. Seit 1794 ist der Garten eng mit Goethe verbunden. Hier befand sich seine „Clausur auf dem Blumen- und Pflanzenberge". Der mächtige Ginkgobaum am Inspektorhaus wurde im Auftrag Goethes gepflanzt, für ihn war das Ginkgoblatt Symbol der Freundschaft und Liebe.

The second oldest of its kind in Germany, the university's botanical garden started life in 1586. Today it contains about 12,000 plants from all the different climatic zones. An arboretum, alpine garden and greenhouse with a cactus house, palm house and an orchid house, are just some of the many attractions here. It is also worth visiting the Victoria house with its prize specimen, the Amazonian giant water lily ("Victoria") with its unusually large leaves. Since 1794 the garden has been closely associated with the great writer and philosopher Goethe. The vast ginkgo tree near the "Inspektorhaus" where Goethe lived during his time in Jena, was planted on his instructions.

Goethe-Gedenkstätte

Das einstige Inspektorhaus des Botanischen Gartens ist heute Goethe-Gedenkstätte. Memorialräume erinnern an das Wirken des Geheimrates. Mit botanischen Studien und dichterischer Muse verbrachte er unzählige Stunden hier, abgeschieden von Zwängen am Weimarer Hof. Goethe weilte insgesamt mehr als fünf Jahre in Jena, förderte die Uni und ging seiner Leidenschaft für die Naturwissenschaften nach. Er führte anatomische Studien durch und fand den Zwischenkiefernknochen beim Menschen.

The former "Inspektorhaus" in the Botanical Garden is now the Goethe Memorial and a series of rooms commemorate the life and work of the great man. Goethe spent many hours here pursuing his botanical studies (or his poetic muse) far from his ministerial duties at the Weimar court. Altogether Goethe spent more than five years in Jena, actively promoting the university and indulging his passion for the natural sciences. He also carried out numerous anatomical studies and was the first to discover the intermaxillary bone in humans.

Griesbachgarten

Das spätbarocke Sommerhaus mit Landschaftsgarten, 1785 für den Theologen Johann Jakob Griesbach errichtet, erwarb der Weimarer Hof 1818 für die russische Großfürstin und Weimarer Großherzogin Mar a Pawlowna. Prinzessinnenschlösschen wird es genannt, weil hier ihre Töchter, die Weimarer Prinzessinnen Augusta und Marie, erzogen und von Goethe unterrichtet wurden. Als Dank ließ Maria Pawlowna im Park das weltweit erste Goethe-Denkmal errichten.

This charming late-Baroque summer residence and landscaped garden, built in 1785 for the theologian Johann Jakob Griesbach, was acquired the Court of Weimar in 1818 for use by the Russian Grand Duchess and the Weimar Grand Duchess Maria Pawlowna. It is often known as the "Little Princesses' Palace", because their daughters, the Weimar princesses Augusta and Marie, grew up here. They were taught by Goethe and, as a token of his thanks for the poet's services, Pawlowna had a monument to the great poet erected here – the first of its kind in the world.

Zeiss-Planetarium

Abenteuerliche visuelle Reisen ins Weltall für Groß und Klein – im dienstältesten und heute auch modernsten Planetarium der Welt ist dies möglich. Jena ist der geistige Geburtsort des modernen Projektionsplanetariums. Der geniale Erfinder und Konstrukteur des „Wunders aus Jena" war Zeiss-Chefingenieur Dr. Walter Bauersfeld. Die 1926 eröffnete 23-Meter-Kuppel des berühmten Zeiss-Planetariums ist heute Jenas Touristenmagnet Nr. 1. Das Großplanetarium zeigt vielseitige pädagogische und musikalische Programme für die ganze Familie. Das Sternentheater entführt in die unendlichen Weiten des Universums und veranschaulicht Phänomene des Sternenhimmels und der Astronomie. Dank neuester Laser-Ganzkuppelprojektion ist im Zeiss-Planetarium der Kosmos voll bewegter Bilder zu erleben. Gigantische Multimedia-Lasershows garantieren fantastische Unterhaltung im 3D-Soundsystem.

Exciting visual journeys into space for visitors of all ages – that is what visitors to the famous Zeiss Planetarium can look forward to. One of the "Wonders of Jena", this is the oldest still-functioning planetarium in the world and nowadays the most modern. Jena is the spiritual birthplace of modern planetarium projection and this fine example was conceived and constructed by Zeiss' brilliant chief engineer, Dr. Walter Bauersfeld. Since it opened in 1926, the planetarium, with its impressive 23-metre high dome, has been Jena's biggest tourist attraction and offers a varied programme of educational and musical events for the whole family. From their comfortable seat in the auditorium visitors are magically 'transported' into the infinite expanse of the universe. With fully-moving images created using the very latest full-dome laser projection technology, the Zeiss Planetarium gives visitors the chance to experience the cosmos at first hand, while vast multi-media laser shows – complete with 3D sound – guarantee unforgettable entertainment for all ages.

Romantikerhaus

Große Geister lebten und wirkten Ende des 18. Jahrhunderts in Jena. Das Literaturmuseum der deutschen Frühromantik zeigt den kultur- und geistesgeschichtlichen Hintergrund für den Aufbruch einer jungen Generation Dichter, Literaturkritiker, Philosophen und Naturwissenschaftler. Im heutigen Romantikerhaus wohnte der Philosoph Johann Gottlieb Fichte, um den sich eine Gruppe scharte, die Jena zum Mittelpunkt frühromantischer Dichtung und Geselligkeit werden ließ. Die Brüder Schlegel, ihre Frauen, Tieck, Novalis, Brentano und Hölderlin entwickelten ihren alternativen Lebensentwurf. Ein Salon mit Theaterbühne lädt die Besucher in die Welt der Romantiker ein.

Many great thinkers lived and worked in Jena at the end of the 18th century. This literary museum of German early Romanticism explores the cultural and intellectual influences behind the emergence of a young generation of poets, literary critics, philosophers and natural scientists. The "Romantikerhaus" was once the home of the philosopher Johann Gottlieb Fichte and it was here that the first proponents of Romanticism gathered to socialise and discuss their ideas, hence Jena's emergence as a centre for early Romantic poetry. Key figures such as the Schlegel brothers (and their wives), Tieck, Novalis, Brentano and Hölderlin made their home in the city, pursuing what would have been considered an alternative lifestyle.

Schillers Gartenhaus

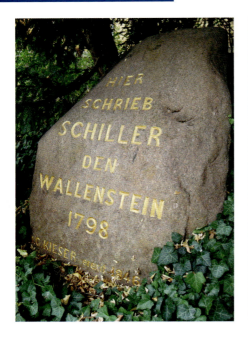

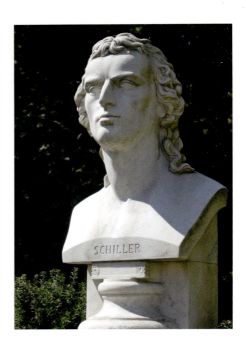

Das Gartenhaus am Schillergässchen ist die einzig erhaltene Wohnstätte Friedrich Schillers in Jena. Nach historischem Vorbild gestaltet, besitzt der idyllische Garten den „genius loci" (Geist des Ortes). Das authentische Kleinod ist eine Oase der Ruhe. In seiner Gartenzinne bearbeitete Schiller im Austausch mit Goethe den „Wallenstein" und schrieb im Wettstreit mit ihm seine berühmten Balladen. Oft saßen beide unter der Laube am ovalen Steintisch.

The summer house on Schillergässchen is the only surviving house occupied by Schiller during his time in Jena. Laid out in the style of the period and perfectly encapsulating the "genius loci", or spirit of this remarkable place, the idyllic garden is a real oasis of calm. It was here in his little garden retreat that Schiller worked on his play "Wallenstein" – with the encouragement of Goethe – and on his famous ballads, in competition with him. The two men were often seen sitting together at an oval stone table under the pergola.

Schiller und Goethe schlossen 1794 ihren Freundschaftsbund in Jena. Das Sommerdomizil Schillers ab 1797, einst vor den Toren der Stadt gelegen, heute eine grüne Insel in verkehrsreicher Citylage, beherbergt Arbeitszimmer, Salon und Schlafkämmerchen. An keinem anderen Ort hielt sich der Dichter so lange auf wie in Jena, diese zehn Jahre gehörten zu seinen produktivsten. In seinem Gartenhaus wird Schillers Geist wieder lebendig.

Schiller and Goethe sealed their bond of friendship in Jena in 1794. Schiller's summer residence – his home from 1797 – once lay outside the city gates. Today, it is a green oasis amid the traffic of a busy city. The poet spent longer in Jena than anywhere else, and these ten years were among his most productive. This delightful summer house brings the spirit of the poet very much to life.

KulturArena

Das Theaterhaus ist die „kreativste Ruine Deutschlands". Hier inszeniert ein kleines Ensemble experimentelles Gegenwartstheater.
Im Sommer lockt die KulturArena zum größten kulturellen Treffpunkt hierzulande auf den Theatervorplatz. Seit mehr als 20 Jahren hat sich das internationale Open-Air-Musikfestival zu einem der längsten, vielfältigsten und erfolgreichsten in Deutschland entwickelt. Sieben Wochen lang, im Juli und August, wird Weltmusik vom Feinsten geboten. Eingeleitet von einem fantasievollen viertägigen Theaterspektakel, gehören auch die FilmArena mit Kurzfilmnacht und die KinderArena, bei der sich die Jüngsten tummeln können, zu dem Festival. Das Amphitheater umweht ein einzigartiges Flair. Tausende Besucher lassen sich von der besonderen Atmosphäre verzaubern. Ganz verschiedene Menschen, Musiken und Kulturen treffen aufeinander. Die KulturArena steht für entspannte Sommerabende im Kreis von Freunden bei guter Musik aus Europa und fernen Kontinenten.

Jena's "Theaterhaus" theatre is sometimes affectionately described as "Germany's most creative ruin" where a small ensemble puts on some experimental contemporary theatre. In summer the theatre forecourt is packed with crowds who flock here to enjoy one of the city's great cultural highlights – the KulturArena festival. This international open-air music festival, which has taken place here for over 20 years, is now one of the longest, most diverse and successful events of its kind in Germany. For an incredible seven weeks throughout July and August, this is the place to hear some of the very best in world music. Opening with a fantastic four-day theatrical spectacular, the festival's many other attractions include the FilmArena, featuring a short film night, and the KinderArena – perfect entertainment for younger festival-goers. On summer evenings the KulturArena provides a relaxed setting for friends to get together and enjoy great music from Europe and further afield.

Phyletisches Museum

Die Jugendstilfassade zeigt im „Lebensbaum" die von Ernst Haeckel geprägten Begriffe Ontogenie und Phylogenie. Der Zoologe hatte die Idee, die darwinsche Abstammungslehre zu veranschaulichen und regte den Museumsbau an. Als Teil des Uni-Instituts für Spezielle Zoologie und Evolutionsbiologie zeigt es die stammesgeschichtliche Entwicklung der Organismen und des Menschen sowie Evolutionsprozesse. Belege nahezu aller Tiergruppen liefern wertvolle Daten zur Verbreitung der Arten.

The "Tree of Life" on the museum's Art Nouveau facade depicts the concepts of ontogeny and phylogeny with which the eminent zoologist Ernst Haeckel was closely associated. He founded this museum because he wanted to explain Darwin's Theory of Evolution. Now part of the University of Jena's Institute for Systematic Zoology and Evolutionary Biology, it continues to explore the phylogenetic development of organisms and explain evolutionary processes.

In der Eingangshalle grüßt ein 100 Jahre alter Gorilla. Das historische Präparat kannte schon Haeckel. Kulturhistorisch wichtig ist das unter Goethes Leitung 1821 in Thüringen geborgene Skelett des fossilen „Urstiers".

Your first sight on entering the museum is a huge gorilla – over 100 years old. Also of great historic and cultural significance is the Thuringian "fossil bull", discovered and described by Goethe in 1821.

Ernst-Haeckel-Haus

Im ehemaligen Wohnhaus Ernst Haeckels (1834–1919) in der Berggasse wird das Leben und Wirken des Jenaer Zoologen erlebbar. Liebevoll wird das Anwesen „Villa Medusa" genannt. Schmuckvoll sind Zimmerdecken mit Zeichnungen der niederen Meerestiere ausgestattet. Haeckel war einer der bekanntesten Wissenschaftler an der Universität. Der darwinistischen Evolutionstheorie verhalf der Naturforscher in kurzer Zeit auch in Deutschland zum Durchbruch. Bis zum Lebensende blieb er Dozent und Professor in Jena.

Once the home of Jena zoologist Ernst Haeckel (1834–1919), the affectionately named "Villa Medusa" in Berggasse is now a museum devoted to the great man's life and work. Haeckel was one of the university's best-known scientists and is credited with helping to popularise Darwin's Theory of Evolution in Germany. He continued to work as a lecturer and professor in Jena until his death.

Seine „Villa Medusa" verkaufte Ernst Haeckel 1918 an die Carl-Zeiss-Stiftung, damit sie als Museum für seinen wissenschaftlichen und künstlerischen Nachlass genutzt wird. Arbeitszimmer und Wohnräume sind in ursprünglichem Zustand mit Mobiliar, Zeichnungen und Schriften erhalten. Man hat den Eindruck, der Hausherr könnte den Raum jeden Moment wieder betreten ...

In 1918 Ernst Haeckel sold his "Villa Medusa" to the Carl Zeiss Foundation for use as a museum for future generations of scientists and artists. His study and living rooms have been preserved just as they were in Haeckel's day, his furnishings, drawings and writings faithfully preserved. You almost feel that the master of the house could walk in at any minute ...

Optisches Museum

Das einzigartige naturwissenschaftlich-technische Museum beherbergt kulturgeschichtliche Meilensteine der Optik aus fünf Jahrhunderten. Eine der bedeutendsten Brillensammlungen Europas, die Laterna magica, faszinierende Hologramme: Im Optischen Museum ist menschliche Erfindungsgabe in Foto-, Fernrohroptik, Mikroskopie und Planetariumstechnik zu erleben. Es gibt Einblicke in das Wirken der Optikpioniere Carl Zeiss, Ernst Abbe und Otto Schott, die den Grundstein für den optischen Präzisionsgerätebau in Jena legten. Die „Historische Zeiss-Werkstatt 1866" mit Laden und Kontor ist lebensnah nachempfunden. Die einzige „lebendige" historische Werkstatt der Optik dokumentiert anschaulich, wie Carl Zeiss handwerklich mühselig Mikroskope fertigte.

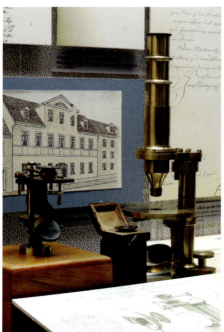

This unique scientific and technical museum documents five centuries of cultural and historical landmarks in the development of optics. With one of the biggest collections of spectacles in Europe, the "laterna magica" and fascinating holograms, the Optical Museum gives visitors a fascinating glimpse of man's progress in the fields of photography, telescopy, microscopy and planetarium technology. In particular, it offers an insight into the work of the optical pioneers Carl Zeiß, Ernst Abbe and Otto Schott, who pioneered optical precision engineering in Jena. The "Historic Zeiss Workshop 1866", complete with offices and a shop, has been realistically recreated to show the laborious techniques Zeiss would have used in producing his microscopes.

Optik zum Anfassen. Die spannende Welt der Lichtwissenschaft können Kinder auf spielerische Weise erforschen. Optische Täuschungen z.B. in einem Spiegelkasten sind eine faszinierende Sache. Themenführungen gibt es auch zu Lichtphänomenen und Raritäten wie Laterna Magica, Guckkasten oder Stereoskop. Das Optische Museum der Ernst-Abbe-Stiftung ist eine wahre Schatzkammer.

Experiencing the world of optics hands-on. Kids can explore the exciting world of light technology through a series of fun activities and are sure to be intrigued by, for example, optical illusions produced using a mirror box. There are also themed tours on different light phenomena and unique rarities such as the "laterna magica", peep-shows and the stereoscope. The Ernst Abbe Foundation's Optical Museum is a real treasure trove.

Ernst-Abbe-Denkmal

Den Carl-Zeiss-Platz am Volkshaus dominiert ein Denkmaltypus europäischen Ranges: das Monument für Ernst Abbe, den Physiker, Industriellen und Sozialreformer. Der zu Ehren des Mitbegründers der Carl-Zeiss-Werke 1911 eingeweihte Pavillon ist das Gemeinschaftswerk dreier Künstler. Bemerkenswert ist seine künstlerische Ausstattung. Schöpfer des achtseitigen, tempelartigen Baues mit vier Portalen und Lichtkuppel ist der belgische Architekt Henry van de Velde. Sein Landsmann Constantin Meunier entwarf zu den Themen Arbeit, Ackerbau, Bergbau, Industrie und Handel vier Bronzereliefs, die an den Wänden eingelassen sind. In der Mitte des Innenraumes steht die von Max Klinger geschaffene, marmorne Herme mit der Büste Abbes.

Carl-Zeiss-Platz near the Volkshaus is dominated by a memorial which has become famous throughout Europe. It commemorates the physicist, industrialist and social reformer Ernst Abbe, who was also co-founder of the Carl Zeiss works. The memorial pavilion, inaugurated in 1911, was the work of three artists and is exquisitely decorated. The creator of this remarkable temple-like, octagonal structure with its four portals and domed roof light, was the Belgian architect Henry van de Velde. Lining the wall are four bronze reliefs – representing the themes of work, farming, mining, industry and trade – designed by his fellow countryman Constantin Meunier. In the centre of the interior stands a marble herm, the work of sculptor Max Klinger, supporting a bust of Abbe.

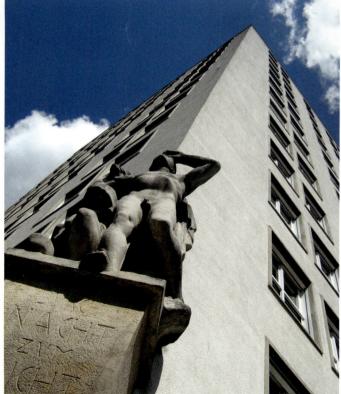

Blickfang am Ernst-Abbe-Hochhaus ist die Plastik „Durch Nacht zum Licht". Das 66 Meter hohe, frühere Zeiss-Hochhaus ist heute Sitz der Jenoptik AG, die sich aus dem Zeiss-Werk ab 1991 erfolgreich zum weltweit agierenden Technologiekonzern mit Licht als Zukunftstechnologie entwickelte.

An eye-catching feature of the high-rise building known as the "Ernst-Abbe-Hochhaus" is the sculpture "Durch Nacht zum Licht" (Through the Night to the Light). This 66-metre high structure, once part of the Zeiss factory complex, is today the headquarters of the optical systems company, Jenoptik AG, established in 1991 as a descendant of the original Zeiss Company. Jenoptik is now a major global optoelectronics company.

Volkshaus

Der elegante Jugendstil-Saal im Volkshaus besticht durch eine ausgezeichnete Akustik. Thüringens größte Konzertorgel besitzt 4.850 klingende Pfeifen und 61 Register. Einst gab der berühmte Komponist Max Reger hier Konzerte. Die 1934 gegründete Jenaer Philharmonie mit dem Philharmonischen Chor hat im Volkshaus ihre Wirkungsstätte. Das Konzertorchester ist international renommiert. Glanzlicht der Vereine ist das Tanztheater, das die Bauhaus-Symbole Kreis, Dreieck, Quadrat präsentiert.

The elegant great hall of the Art Nouveau-style "Volkshaus", where the famous composer Max Reger once gave concerts, is known for its excellent acoustics. It also has Thuringia's largest concert organ with 4,850 pipes and 61 registers. The Volkshaus is also home to the Jenaer Philharmonie orchestra (and its affiliated Philharmonic Choir), founded in 1934. This fine concert orchestra has gained a distinguished reputation over the years. Another cultural highlight is the work of the Dance Theatre.

Das stattliche Volkshaus atmet Kultur in architektonischer Schönheit. Auf Initiative Ernst Abbes wurde es 1903 mit den Mitteln der Carl-Zeiss-Stiftung als Veranstaltungshaus und Lesehalle für alle Bürger zur „Verbreitung von Bildung unter dem Volke" erbaut. Es besitzt ein großes, stilvolles Foyer und beherbergt die Ernst-Abbe-Bücherei. Das Volkshaus ist kultureller Mittelpunkt der Stadt.

A fine building of great architectural merit, the Volkshaus exudes culture. It was built in 1903 on the initiative of Ernst Abbe and funded by the Carl Zeiss Foundation as an event venue and public reading room for the purpose of "bringing education to the masses". It has a spacious and stylish foyer and also houses the Ernst Abbe Library. The Volkshaus provides the ideal focal point for Jena's cultural scene.

Campus Ernst-Abbe-Platz

Der Ernst-Abbe-Platz, neuer Campus der Universität, ist seit 1996 geprägt von Stahlskulpturen des weltbekannten New Yorker Künstlers Frank Stella. Der „Schrott aus Amerika" sorgte für einen Aufschrei. Als Symbol des einstigen Industriequartiers Zeiss-Hauptwerk geben sie eine Vorstellung vom Wandel, der in Jena erlitten und bewältigt wurde. Heute versprüht das studentische Flair viel Charme. Abgüsse antiker Statuen im Foyer der Universität bilden mit der modernen Architektur eine kontrastreiche Einheit. Auf dem Platz steht übrigens Deutschlands erstes Hochhaus. 1915 in Stahlskelettbauweise für Zeiss errichtet, misst es 43 Meter. Eigentlich wollte sein Architekt einen 100 Meter hohen Wolkenkratzer nach Vorbild der Chicagoer Schule bauen, der damals aber nicht genehmigt wurde.

Since 1996 the university's new campus on Ernst-Abbe-Platz has been graced with a series of steel sculptures by the world-renowned New York artist Frank Stella. Not to everyone's taste, his abstract "garbage from America" has been the subject of much controversy. Symbolising the former industrial works of the Zeiss Corporation, the five sculptures represent the transformation which Jena has undergone and the turbulent times it has lived through. Today this area is a bustling student hub. Replicas of ancient statues in the university's foyer provide an interesting contrast to the modern architecture of the buildings. Ernst Abbe Platz is also the site of Germany's first high-rise building – a steel frame structure, built for Zeiss in 1915, which reaches a height of 43 metres.

Goethe Galerie

Auf historischem Boden, umrandet von denkmalgeschützten Teilen des früheren Zeiss-Hauptwerkes, entstand 1996 das Atrium-Hotel „Esplanade" und die architektonisch attraktive Einkaufspassage „Goethe Galerie". Ihrem Slogan „Alles außer gewöhnlich" macht sie alle Ehre.

Occupying a historic site close to sections of the historic former Zeiss works, the "Esplanade" atrium hotel and the adjoining "Goethe Galerie" shopping centre were built in 1996. The centre certainly lives up to its slogan of providing shoppers with "everything but the ordinary".

Die „Goethe Galerie" ist ein bauliches Meisterwerk, Tradition und Zeitgeist in faszinierender Symbiose vereinend. Ein gläsernes Schmuckstück ist die Rotunde. Hier weitet sich das alles überspannende Glasdach zur imposanten Kuppel mit 55 Metern Durchmesser. Beliebter Treffpunkt ist der historische Zeiss-Sternenprojektor Cosmorama.

The "Goethe Galerie" is acknowledged as an architectural masterpiece, a fascinating symbiosis of traditional and contemporary. A particularly attractive feature is its glass rotunda, a vast and impressive domed roof measuring 55 metres across. The historic Zeiss Cosmorama star projector is a popular meeting place.

Kneipenmeile Wagnergasse

In der Wagnergasse, dem alten Handwerkerviertel der Wagenschmiede im mittelalterlichen Vorort Leutra, ist zu jeder Tageszeit was los, vor allem allabendlich. Dann avanciert sie zum Treffpunkt fürs Nachtleben. Jenas bunte Kneipenmeile ist von magischer Anziehungskraft, aufgeschlossen, multikulturell. Urige Kneipen, Bars und charmante Straßencafés reihen sich aneinander. Das Szenecafé „Stilbruch" in urgemütlicher Atmosphäre gehört zu den beliebtesten. Hier ist zu spüren, was einst Studenten schon sangen: „Und in Jene lebt sich's bene" – in Jena lebt sich's gut. Durch die Gasse verlief einst die Hauptstraße nach Weimar.

Originally the blacksmiths' quarter of the medieval suburb of Leutra, the Wagnergasse is always a bustling place, but it is at night that the place really comes alive. Jena's vibrant 'pub mile' has a magical charm all of its own and a uniquely cosmopolitan, multi-cultural atmosphere. There is no shortage of friendly pubs, bars and street cafés – a particular favourite is the trendy "Stilbruch" restaurant, renowned for its cosy ambience and great food. Here you can really appreciate the words of the old student song: "Und in Jene lebt sich's bene" (Life is good in Jena)! At one time the main route to Weimar passed through this narrow street.

Am Johannisplatz steht die Skulptur „Ergo Bibamus" – drum lasset uns trinken! Ein fröhlich zechender Student reitet auf einem Bierfass, aus dessen Spundloch der Bierteufel kommt, der ihn zum Trinken verführt hat. Die Plastik erinnert an das Akademische Brau- und Schankrecht in Jena. Das Brauhaus bestand von 1594 bis 1903 neben dem Anatomieturm.

Worth taking a look at on Johannisplatz is the sculpture entitled "Ergo Bibamus" (therefore let us drink!). This interesting piece, which depicts a carousing student sitting astride a beer barrel, trying to outdrink the devil, commemorates Jena's acquisition of the right to brew and sell beer. The original brewery stood next to the Anatomy Tower from 1594 to 1903.

Schott-Villa und Glasmuseum

Wo Otto Schott 1884 das „Glastechnische Laboratorium" gründete, sind im Schott GlasMuseum Meilensteine der Produkt- und Technologiegeschichte multimedial zu erleben. „Jenaer Glas"-Designklassiker ist die Wagenfeld-Teekanne. Das facettenreiche Lebenswerk des bedeutenden Wissenschaftlers und Unternehmers spiegelt sich in der Schott-Villa wider. Das einstige Wohnhaus des Glaspioniers zeigt Firmengeschichte, Industriefotografie und Sonderausstellungen wie Glasskulpturen des in Jena gebürtigen Künstlers Gerd Sonntag als glaspoetische Hommage an die Stadt.

Established in 1884, Otto Schott's former "glass technology laboratory" has today become the Schott Glass Museum, offering a multimedia exploration of important milestones in the history of glass production. The Wagenfeld teapot is a "Jena Glass" design classic. Visitors to the Schott Villa, once the home of this famous glass pioneer, can learn all about the life and work of a man who was both an influential scientist and an entrepreneur. There is a wealth of information on the history of the Schott company, industry photographs and special exhibitions, such as the collection of glass sculptures by the Jena artist Gerd Sonntag.

Antikensammlungen

Das frühere Archäologische Museum der Uni mit eindrucksvollen Abgüssen antiker Großplastiken hat eine neue Heimstatt. Die Antikensammlungen zeigen Statuen, Büsten, Reliefs, Vasen, Kleinbronzen, Terrakotten sowie Statuetten aus Hochkulturen des antiken Mittelmeerraumes, von der mykenischen bis in die römische Zeit. Zu den Schätzen gehören ägyptische Mumien und trojanische Funde aus dem Nachlass von Heinrich Schliemann.

The former archaeological museum of Jena University, with its impressive replica antique sculptures, now has a new home. The collection features statues, busts, reliefs, vases, miniature bronzes, terracotta and statuettes from the advanced civilisations of the ancient mediterranean region. Among the many priceless treasures on display are Egyptian mummies and Trojan finds bequeathed by Heinrich Schliemann.

Paradies und Saale

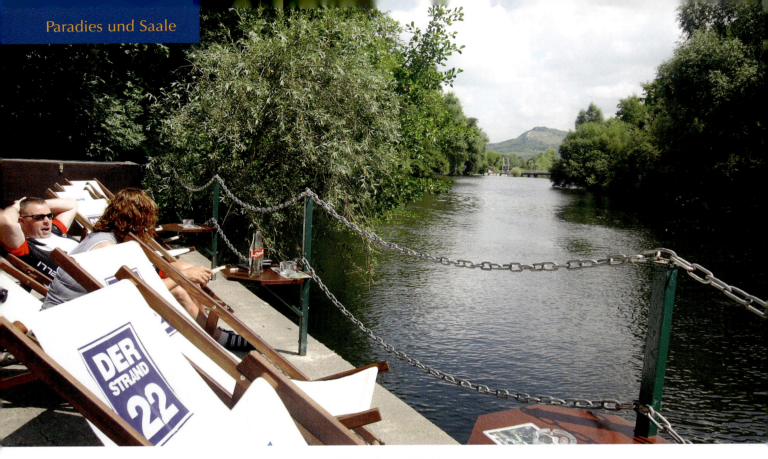

Entlang der sich 17 Kilometer durch die Stadt schlängelnden Saale führen vom ICE-Bahnhof Jena-Paradies zentrumsnah Wege direkt ins Paradies und den Volkspark Oberaue. Die paradiesische Auenlandschaft ist eine Freizeitoase zum Seele baumeln lassen. In der Zeit des Jenaer Herzogtums (1672–1690) war das Paradies ein Lust- und Wandelgarten. Studenten und Gelehrte flanierten hier, später auch Goethe. Im Sommer eröffnet sich von der „Strandbar 22" am Saaleufer ein schöner Blick auf den Jenzig.

Following the river Saale as it winds along its 17 kilometre route, a number of paths lead from the central ICE railway station (aptly-named Paradies) to the area of the same name and the popular 'Volkspark Oberaue'. The idyllic meadowland countryside here provides the perfect setting for leisure activities of all kinds. During the Duchy of Saxe-Jena (1672–1690) the Paradies was a popular pleasure garden, a place where students and scholars would come for a leisurely stroll – Goethe himself was a frequent visitor. In summer a seat at the "Strandbar 22" beside the Saale affords wonderful views of Jenzig Mountain.

Mitten im Paradies kreuzen sich die Fern-Radwanderwege „Thüringer Städtekette" und „Saale-Radweg". Reizvoll ist auch das Paddeln auf der Saale. Mit Kanu, Floß oder Schlauchboot können Wasserwanderer die einzigartige Flusslandschaft erkunden. Die zentrale Einstiegstelle befindet sich am Gries.

Two long-distance cycle paths (the "Saale-Radweg") cross at the centre of Paradies Park or, for something a bit more sedate, it is also possible to hire a paddle boat on the river. Those keen to explore the unique river landscape properly have the option of taking out a canoe, raft or inflatable dinghy – these are available at 'am Gries'.

Mühltal und Forst

Der Brau-Gasthof „Papiermühle" am westlichen Stadtrand knüpft an die Brautradition an, die seit 1332 in Jena belegt ist. Führungen durch die Hausbrauerei gestatten einen unterhaltsamen Ausflug in die Welt der Brauhandwerkskunst mit Verkostung des beliebten Burschenpils, „Alt-Jenaer" und Schellenbiers. Die Sommerlinde im idyllischen Hof ist schon mehr als 500 Jahre alt.

The "Papiermühle" restaurant on the city's western edge is a reminder of a brewing tradition in Jena which can be traced right back to 1332. A tour of its home brewery is an entertaining way to learn about the craft of brewing beer – including, naturally, a chance to sample the popular "Alt-Jenaer Burschenpils" or "Schellenbier". Look out for the summer lime growing in the charming courtyard here – it is over 500 years old.

Der Grenzstein mit Weinrebe erinnert an den Jenaer Weinanbau. Rund um die Stadt wuchs im Mittelalter viel Wein, mag dessen Ruhm auch manchmal zweifelhaft gewesen sein, nach Luthers Worten über Jena, „wo der Essig wächst". Am Südhang über dem Mühltal gelangt der Wanderer zum Sandsteinfelsen „Lutherkanzel".

A boundary stone with a carved vine motif is a reminder of Jena's wine-growing heritage. Back in the Middle Ages there were many vineyards around Jena, though the quality of the wine produced may not always have been of the best. Luther is said to have described Jena as the place "where the vinegar grows".

Bismarckturm und Frauenschuh

Im Forst erinnert der Bismarckturm von 1909 an den Besuch des Reichskanzlers 1892 in Jena. Von hier aus kann man eine herrliche Aussicht auf die Sonnenberge, den Landgrafen und weit über die Stadt genießen. Kalkflora lässt hier 27 Wildorchideenarten gedeihen, darunter der „Frauenschuh". Jena beheimatet fast die Hälfte aller Arten in Europa. Diese Orchideenvielfalt ist in Deutschland einzigartig.

The "Bismarckturm" in Jena forest (built in 1909) commemorates the Chancellor's visit to Jena in 1892. Natural landmarks to look out for include the Sonnenberge and the Landgrafen and, on a clear, you can also see far beyond the city. Jena has an unusually high density of orchids – over 27 species are to be found here, including the exquisite "lady's slipper" – in fact, almost half of all wild orchid species in Europe grow here. This diversity is unique within Germany.

Sonnenberge mit Landgrafen

Vom Mühltal aus aufsteigend verläuft ein schmaler Horizontalweg entlang dem schroffen Muschelkalkhang der Sonnenberge. Der Blick auf die Stadt ist spätnachmittags besonders schön. Bald ist der Landgrafen mit dem 30 Meter hohen Aussichtsturm erreicht – der „Balkon Jenas". Über die Bergkante ragt das gläserne Restaurant, kontrastierend zum Natursteinbau. Das Landgrafenhaus von 1891 ist wieder ein Schmuckstück. Der Name stammt wohl von den früheren Weinbergen der Landgrafen.

A narrow horizontal path leads out of the Mühl Valley along the rugged fossil-flecked limestone slopes of the Sonnenberge. For particularly stunning views of the city, late afternoon is definitely the best time to come. From here it is not far to Landgrafen Mountain with its viewing platform – the locals call it the "the balcony of Jena". The glass restaurant looking over the edge provides a stark contrast to the natural stone of the buildings all around. Dating from 1891, the "Landgrafenhaus" is well worth a visit.

Jenaer Balkon

Die schönste Aussicht auf die Stadt, die Kernberge und ins Saaletal bis zur Leuchtenburg verlieh dem stadtnahen Landgrafenplateau die Bezeichnung „Jenaer Balkon". Vom Türmchen der Gaststätte „Landgrafen" und von den Terrassen aus sind fantastische Panoramablicke möglich. Über die mehr als 300 Stufen des Landgrafenstiegs gelangt man am schnellsten hierher.

The nickname "Balcony of Jena" is a particularly apposite description of the Landgrafen plateau – from here the views of the city, Kernberge mountains and the Saale Valley as far as Leuchtenburg, are unsurpassed. From the little tower of the "Landgrafen" restaurant and the terraces the panorama is fantastic – well worth climbing over 300 steps to experience!

Cospeda mit Napoleonstein

Hier wurde europäische Geschichte geschrieben. Auf dem Windknollen oberhalb Jenas erinnert der Napoleonstein an die verheerende Schlacht zwischen Franzosen und Preußen bei Jena und Auerstedt am 14. Oktober 1806. In Cospeda beherbergt „Der Grüne Baum zur Nachtigall" die Gedenkstätte „Museum 1806", die die Geschichte und den Verlauf der Doppelschlacht im Diorama mit Zinnfiguren veranschaulicht. Napoleons Truppen besiegten die Armee der Preußen, mehr als 30.000 Tote und Verwundete gab es. Alle fünf Jahre stellen Traditionsvereine aus Europa die Schlacht ohne Blutvergießen nach. Zum 200. Jahrestag 2006 (rechts) trugen 1.800 Menschen aus 18 Nationen zur Völkerverständigung bei. Historiker Mark Schneider (USA) spielte Bonaparte ziemlich überzeugend.

European history was made on this site. On the highest part of the Landgrafenberg – the "Windknollen" – above Jena, the 'Napoleonstein' (Napoleon Stone) commemorates the devastating battle fought between the French and the Prussians at Jena and Auerstedt. The "Grüne Baum zur Nachtigall" in Cospeda also houses the "Museum 1806" where a diorama with tin soldiers recounts the story of this famous double battle. Napoleon's troops defeated the Prussian army but the human cost was great, with over 30,000 soldiers dead or wounded. These days the only battles are bloodless ones. Every five years re-enactment societies from all over Europe come here to recreate the battle. In 2006, a total of 1,800 people from 18 countries came together to commemorate the 200th anniversary of this historic event (right). The part of Bonaparte was played – quite convincingly – by the American historian Mark Schneider.

Historisches Schlachtfeld 1806

Goethepark Drackendorf

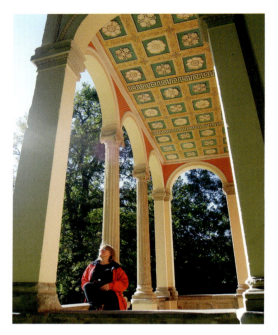

Johann Wolfgang von Goethe wandelte oft durch diesen Park, als Gast des Freiherrn von Ziegesar im Drackendorfer Gut. Mit dessen junger Tochter Silvie verband ihn eine Romanze. Den altrömischen Pavillon ließ Gutsbesitzerin Clara von Helldorff 1854 nach einer Italienreise bauen. Seine Tradition als Teehäuschen lebt in dem restaurierten Kleinod durch literarisch-musikalische Teestunden des Heimatvereins auf.

Johann Wolfgang von Goethe often walked in this park whilst staying as a guest of the Baron von Ziegesar at Drackendorf. And it was here that he also enjoyed a romantic dalliance with the baron's young daughter, Silvie. The Roman-style pavilion was built in 1854 for the lady of the house Clara von Helldorff on her return from a trip to Italy. Now beautifully restored, this little gem of a building has once again been returned to its original function as a place to take tea – fittingly, the local history society organise regular literary-musical tea parties here.

Lobdeburg

Die Lobdeburg, Gründungsburg der Stadt Jena, auf einem Bergsporn über Lobeda, ist bauhistorisch wertvoll als Symbol romanischen Burgenbaus von 1166. Reste mit Palas und Kapellenerker lassen die Ausmaße des Stammsitzes der aus Franken gekommenen Herren von Lobdeburg erkennen. Sie haben um 1240 dem bis dato unbedeutenden Ort Jena das Stadtrecht verliehen, stehen somit bedeutungsvoll am Anfang der Stadtgeschichte. Die alte Bogenbrücke über die Saale im alten Ortskern Burgau, im Krieg 1945 zerstört, ist nach historischem Vorbild wiedererstanden. Für den Bau Ende des 15. Jahrhunderts waren Natursteine der verfallenen Lobdeburg verwendet worden. Vom idyllischen Biergarten des urigen Lokals Flößerstube „Am Wehr" bietet sich ein reizvoller Blick auf die altehrwürdige Steinbrücke und zum Johannisberg mit seinen imposanten Muschelkalkhängen.

On a mountain spur above Lobeda sits the ruined Lobdeburg Castle from which the city of Jena grew. Dating from 1166, it is a fine of Romanesque-style castle architecture. The only parts of the original building still remaining include the Great Hall and the bay window of the chapel, sufficient to give us a clear idea of the scale of the original castle, once the seat of the Frankish Lords of Lobdeburg. It was they who granted Jena its town charter in 1240. Spanning the river Saale in the district of Burgau is a historic late 15th century arched bridge, constructed using stone from the ruined Lobdeburg. It has now been fully restored following its destruction in 1945. The beer garden of the delightful pub and restaurant "am Wehr" affords excellent views of this fine old bridge and the fossil-flecked limestone slopes of the Johannisberg.

Jenzig

„Sei mir gegrüßt, mein Berg mit dem rötlich strahlenden Gipfel …" Schiller war verzückt vom majestätischen Jenzig, eines der „Sieben Wunder" Jenas, eine geologische Attraktion. Steil aufragend weckt die markante Form des 386 Meter hohen Berges Fantasien, er wird als „Matterhorn" bezeichnet oder „Rigi des Saaletales". Beim Aufstieg sind 200 Höhenmeter zu überwinden. Die Berggaststätte mit Jenas höchstem Biergarten und Panoramaterrasse laden zur Einkehr. Der Wanderweg auf dem „Hufeisen" führt zur Kunitzburg.

"Greetings, my exquisite red-topped mountain …" – the words of the poet Schiller who was completely enchanted by this most majestic of geological wonders – the Jenzig, one of the "Seven Wonders" of Jena. Soaring steeply upwards, the distinctive shape of this 386-metre high mountain has made it the stuff of fantasy and it has been described variously as Jena's "Matterhorn" and the "Rigi of the Saale Valley". Those tackling the 200-metre climb to the top can look forward to a well-deserved rest and some delicious refreshment on the lovely panoramic terrace of Jena's highest beer garden.

Fuchsturm

Über dem Ziegenhainer Tal thront der Fuchsturm, das älteste Wahrzeichen Jenas, letzter Zeuge von Burgenherrlichkeit mit Kaiserpfalz, der ersten deutschen Reichsburg östlich der Saale. Neben dem Bergfried von Kirchberg (Aussicht) lädt hier Jenas älteste Berggaststätte ein.

Enthroned high above the Ziegenhain Valley stands the Fuchsturm (Fox Tower), Jena's oldest landmark, the keep of the first imperial castle in Germany east of the Saale. Next to the keep (an excellent viewing-point) is Jena's oldest mountain restaurant.

Kernberg-Horizontale

450 Kilometer markierte Wanderwege hat Jena. Abwechslungsreich schlängelt sich die „SaaleHorizontale" 72 Kilometer um die Stadt, macht panoramasüchtig! Die Kernberge, einer der schönsten Abschnitte, leuchten von Weitem. An steilen Abbruchkanten einer Muschelkalkplatte, auf mehr als 200 Millionen Jahre altem Meeresgrund, verlaufen spektakulär schmale Wege dicht am Fels und steil abfallenden, schroffen Hängen. Die einzigartige Berglandschaft um Jena zu erwandern, ist eine schöne Herausforderung: grandiose Blicke, Rastplätze, Ausflugslokale gibt es reichlich. Die „SaaleHorizontale" kann in Etappen absolviert werden. Am Fuße der Kernberge beginnt ein geologischer Lehrpfad mit dem Naturdenkmal „Teufelslöcher", einer bizarr gefalteten Felswand mit Höhlen, in denen Fledermäuse leben.

Jena boasts a total of 450 kilometres of hiking trails. One of them, the delightfully varied "SaaleHorizontale" winds its way for 72 kilometres around the city, opening up some irresistible views along the way. One of the prettiest stretches allows you views of the Kernberge mountains in the distance. Incised into the limestone plateau (the seabed 200 million years ago) are spectacular narrow paths which pass close by the rocks and the steep, rugged slopes of this stunning landscape. Exploring the unique mountain landscape around Jena can be quite a challenge at times, but the superb vistas make it all worthwhile and there is no shortage of places to rest and enjoy some well-deserved refreshment. A special 'geological trail' starting at the foot of the Kernberge mountains takes in fascinating natural landmarks such as the "Teufelslöcher" (Devils' Holes).

Wandern mit Weitblick auf Jenas Skyline. Von der mittleren Kernberg-Horizontale aus bietet sich eine fantastische Aussicht mit Alpenfeeling. Geologisch interessant sind die „Studentenrutsche", eine Geröllschneise im Muschelkalkhang, und der Felssturz „Diebeskrippe" in einer Schlucht.

Hiking with the Jena skyline in the distance. The middle section of the Kernberg-Horizontale opens up fantastic, almost alpine views. Interesting geological features include an erosion channel in the limestone slope and the "Diebeskrippe" crevice.

Lichtstadt Jena

Die „Lichtstadt" Jena hat Ausstrahlung. Als „Leuchtturm des Ostens" wird hier Zukunft aus Tradition gestaltet. Die Hightech-Stadt ist Wirtschaftsmetropole Nr. 1 in Thüringen und zählt zu den „Top Ten" der wirtschaftsstärksten Städte in Deutschland. Jena ist eine Stadt mit hoher Lebensqualität.

A truly unique location, Jena – this "City of Light" and an acknowledged "Beacon of the East"- is a place where the future is shaped by the traditions of the past. Not only is it Thuringia's number one economic hub, it is also ranked among the "Top Ten" most economically successful cities in Germany. But Jena is not just an impressive 'high-tech city' – it is also a great place to live!

Stadt der Wissenschaft

„Wissen und Wachsen – made in Jena". Der Stifterverband für die Deutsche Wissenschaft verlieh Jena 2008 den Titel „Stadt der Wissenschaft". Ein Netzwerk aus Vertretern der Wissenschaft, Wirtschaft, Kultur und Stadt befördert Erfinder- und Unternehmergeist. Thüringens größter Wissenschaftscampus Beutenberg mit Max-Planck-, Fraunhofer- und Leibniz-Institut bündelt Forschung auf Weltniveau – ein „Olymp des Wissens". Mit Universität und Ernst-Abbe-Fachhochschule für angewandte Wissenschaften steht Jena für Optik, Optoelektronik, Laser- und Biotechnologie, „global player" Carl Zeiss ist weltweit bekannt, riesig die Begeisterung für Wissenschaft. Die „Lange Nacht der Wissenschaften" gestattet Blicke hinter die Kulissen des Abenteuers Forschung. Von Jenoptik stammen spektakuläre Laserinszenierungen.

"From knowledge comes growth – made in Jena". In 2008, Jena was awarded the title "City of Science" by the "Stifterverband für die Deutsche Wissenschaft" – a network of representatives from the fields of science, business, culture and local government whose aim is to actively promote creativity and entrepreneurship. Thuringia's largest scientific centre, the Beutenberg campus, and the Max Planck-, Fraunhofer- and Leibniz Institutes together provide world-class research facilities. With its Friedrich Schiller University and the Ernst Abbe University, Jena is a "global player" in the world of optics, laser engineering and biotechnology. The "Long Night of the Sciences" is an initiative to encourage the public to come and have a behind-the-scenes look at the adventure that is research and enjoy spectacles such as Jenoptik's spectacular laser displays.

Buchhinweise

Jenaer Tischgeschichten
Eine kulinarische Reise durch fünf Jahrhunderte

Christin Hill und Babara Kösling

ISBN: 978-3-65400-084-5

19,95 € [D]

Jena
Rundgänge durch die Geschichte

Christin Hill, Uta Lörzer, Michael Platen, Fanny Rödenbeck und Helga Spath

ISBN: 978-3-86680-637-5

14,90 € [D]

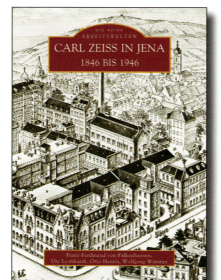

Carl Zeiss in Jena
1846 bis 1946

Otto Haueis, Franz-Ferdinand von Falkenhausen, Ute Leonhardt, Otto Wiegand und Wolfgang Wimmer

ISBN: 978-3-89702-772-5

17,90 € [D]

Weitere Bücher aus Jena finden Sie unter:

www.suttonverlag.de